Business

Ideas for a

Kid

How to Become an Entrepreneur as a Kid

Dave Josephson

ISBN: 9798396695498

1. Introduction

Starting a business as a kid is exciting,! It gives kids the opportunity to learn and acquire many life-long skills early in life and helps them to grow up as responsible individuals
Starting a business helps kids to learn many invaluable life skills. They easily develop important social skills such as negotiating, public speaking, networking, and problem-solving among others.

Specifically, here are some of the great benefits it offers for kids.

.

Learning New Skills – Starting a business early can help provide you with a platform to express yourself creatively and develop important life skills such as problem-solving, effective communication, decision-making, and organization.

Exploring Passions and Interests – Business ownership offers you the opportunity to explore your passions and interests expressively. Additionally, working together gives young ones the chance to realize different perspectives and build empathy.

.   .

Obtaining financial freedom – It gives you a chance to earn money, and the opportunity to gain valuable experience about financial management. It makes kids to gain financial independence as they can learn how to save and invest money.

Supporting The Community – Kids with financial freedom are often at the forefront of helping their community and other people through donations or services.

Gaining Confidence and Self-Esteem – Engaging kids in the world of business at a young age promotes self-confidence and aids in boosting self-esteem.

2. How to Start a Business as a Kid

As you can see, becoming an entrepreneur at a young age comes with many goodies. To succeed, you will need to follow the same business-related rules as when starting a business as an established adult.

For you to be able to do this effectively, you will need to consult your parent or guardian for direction and guidance.

You need to involve them in the process for you to get your business off the ground.

There are certain requirements just as when setting up a grown-up-owned business before you can start your business. This is the area where your parents will probably be of help you.

In addition, you may need to get expert guidance from specialists such as lawyers, accountants, and tax advisors, who would be able to give you proper direction based on your situation. They will be able to see you through the process without much problem.
This book shares basic information that can help you understand many of the things you will need to take care of.
Some of which are discussed below

Decide on the business type you want to start
In this venture, making the right decision is very vital to your success. To succeed, you have to think about the things you love to do

and the things you enjoy and have the natural ability and skills to do in deciding on the type of business you want to start. A good way around this is to see if there is a hobby that you can easily turn into a profitable business. For example, if you enjoy being in the company of pet animals, the pet-sitting business will work out for you. And if you love creativity you can consider producing artwork or jewelry to sell. Or if you enjoy entertaining and caring for small children, babysitting is the best way to go. Perhaps you are strong and fit and enjoy being outdoors; helping homeowners with their lawn work might be a perfect match.

Whatever your choice just make sure it is achievable. The best way is to start with simple things you can do at first then focus, and follow through.

Discuss your interest with your parents

Your parents or guardians are key parts of the whole process. They will guide you to follow the rule so that you don't get yourself into trouble if you fail to follow the rules that apply to normal business settings. Depending on the type of your business and its location, there could be other obligations you may need to satisfy as well. They will guide you properly on how to obtain relevant local licenses or permits to enable you to operate without violating any rules. They will also help you in all other areas such as getting the right customers and fixing the appropriate pricing for your business.

Reach out to your would be customers

Including reaching out to your target customers in your initial plan will help shape your business. It will guide your operation as well as your expectation when you start the business. You will learn about their preferences and how much they are willing to pay for your services.

You can discuss with your parents to help you identify potential customers who will convert well. In searching for customers, for safety reasons don't approach strangers alone, your parent can be of help in this regard.

Instead, you can talk with your friends, trusted adults, and relatives who might become your potential clients.

You might also consider demonstrations of your business ideas to people to get their perspectives.

This feedback will help you to know how to improve your products and services so that you can serve them better.

Develop a Business plan for your business

A business plan includes the logistics of what it will take to start and operate your business. You want to consider the following

· Where you intend to run your business

· Your potential customers (e.g. families, friends, individuals, other children, adults, men, women, etc.)

· What do you need? (tools, and equipment)

· The financial aspects. This includes what amount is required to get you off and run your business. This can be especially challenging but with the help of your parents it becomes easier. They can easily figure out the cost to get you started.

Plan for the legal requirements

You have to plan to manage the legal responsibilities that come with operating a business, This is vital as kid business owners must observe many of the same instructions and legal requirements as adults.

Professionals such as a lawyer and accountants or tax advisors are important resources to help you understand what it is all about. Engage them so that you can make informed decisions and take care of all the necessary details.

Getting Started

Choose a name for your business

This is a crucial aspect of the whole process as this is what will be used to identify your business.

Therefore, your business name must be memorable and reflect what you are doing.

Register your business name and type

Most kid-owned businesses are better registered as sole proprietorships because it's the easiest way to start a business. So, you have to register your name with the appropriate bodies.

Obtain local licenses and permits

You may need county or local business licenses and permits before you can operate.

It will be a good idea to find out about this from relevant authorities before you start selling your products or services.

Open a bank account for your business

Creating a bank account for your business is very vital. This action will help you to keep a record of your business spending and earnings.

It will also make tax reporting time much easier.

When you make profits of more than $400 in a year, you must file an income tax return.

Plan to market your new business

You must plan to market your new business the appropriate modern channels.

There are many options you can employ to market your business and attract customers.

:

· **Website**
· **Email marketing**.
· **Flyers**

3. Guide to Creating a Lemonade Stand

Running a lemonade stand can be one of the most profitable, cost-effective, and popular businesses for kids. It can be a fun way to introduce kids to the entrepreneurial spirit and make some decent money.

It will not only teach valuable lessons about money and customer service to kids but also offer a good summer entertaining activity.

As is the case with most kid business ventures, before you even start considering setting up, you have to make sure it isn't against the rules in your location. It is therefore very important you find out about regulations guiding the setting up of lemonade stands in your area. You need to know if **you're allowed to set**

up a stand and also the requirements. See if it is mandatory for you get a permit or comply with any local laws. In some states, you may need a permit to set up. Some states have no such regulation in place. So, it is important you do your assignment very well. You can ask your parents to seek clarification. Alternatively, you can call your local Business Bureau to get more information. The following guidelines will be very useful in setting up your stand.

Gather your Ingredients

Next, you want to gather your ingredients. Note that using good quality ingredients endears your customers to your business as they will return time and time.

It is equally to also note that people often appreciate the use of fresh ingredients. Try to see if you can get freshly squeezed lemonade to serve your customers.(lemon pix)

However, if it is not possible, a powdered lemonade mix or frozen concentrate can as well work just fine. Try as much as possible to keep your drink cold *in the hot summer sun.* ~~You may have to make available plenty of ice on the day of the sale to keep your drink cold as the drinks won't stay cold for~~ *long,*

In addition to regular lemonade, offering multiple other popular lemons such as pink lemonade or strawberry lemonade will boost your patronage and give you a rewarding experience.

Another best practice for on-the-go lemonade drinking is **prepackaging** the lemonade drink in mason jars. This practice will ensure each customer gets the same amount, it also works well for guiding younger children who may not be able to pour without making messes.

Choose a popular spot. Choosing the right location is crucial to the success of your project. An ideal location will be a busy street or a place that gets a daily decent foot traffic. Intersections or joints are equally good locations since people are passing from more than one direction.

A dead-end street or a place that is tucked away in a corner might not work. However, just make sure the place is safe and secure. In addition, you should avoid setting up in a place that is too close to streets or highways.

Eye-catching Stand

The next thing you'll want to focus on is creating a stand that is attractive to customers. You need to do whatever you can to get the attention of people to your stand. You can build or purchase an actual stand. Whatever your choice, just make sure it is appealing. Bright and bold colors often do the magic.

Another brilliant idea is to add simple but elegant decor items to make the stand eye-catching to your customers. You can decorate your drink dispenser as well.

Timing is crucial

In addition to the good location, correct timing is equally an important factor too. Afternoon, when it's hottest out, might be a good time than a cooler morning or evening. Therefore, you should target midday on weekends or weekdays as anyone outside during the heat of the day is going to need a refreshing drink to stay cool.

Think of a fair price. Often, lemonade stands are either under or overpriced, so make sure you price it right. If it is too expensive no one would buy your products and if it is too cheap, you would barely make any money. However, this mainly depends on how fancy you make your lemonade. Homemade lemonade with fresh ingredients tends to cost more

You could perhaps charge $1.00 to $1.25 per drinking cup. If you're using **lemonade that's been elevated with additions,** people won'tpossinly pay more than $0.25 to $0.50 per cup.

Alternatively, you can make the two options available and adopt a "pay what you want" model.

Figure 1Fresh Lemonades

Make your lemonade stand unique

Another crucial step in the preparation for a successful lemonade stand is inspiring your stand with extras. You have to be creative with your lemonade stand. One of the ways to elevate your lemonade stand is by offering your customers easy grab-and-go snacks.

Fresh mint leaves and lavender are great ingredients you can add to lemonade to create a more unique stand.

You can offer this as a freebie for those who purchase or charge them separately.

Try to make your customers comfortable

Try as much as possible to ensure the comfort of the customers at your stand to make you stand **out.** Once their first visit is pleasant and memorable, they will always want to visit again.

In addition, you can provide some shade, chairs, and foldable tables. Plus a TV or a large tablet for your customers to watch any programs such as sports and games.

Make a big, inviting, and colorful sign to draw people's attention to your stand. It should contain what you're selling and how much it costs. Make it attractive with bright colors and pictures You might want to draw a picture of lemonade to make it visually appealing.

.

Be courteous and appreciative to your customers when you make a sale

In dealing with your customers, make sure you deal with them with good manners. When they want to buy, carefully pour a cup and hand it to them with a napkin. Once they are served, you can then collect their money and place it in your cash register. Don't forget to appreciate your customers, saying "thank you' will go a long way to appease them.

Figure2 homemade lemonades with fresh ingredients

4. Dog Walking Business

Figure 3Dog Walking

Another kids-friendly business is the Dog walking business.

Dogs are perceived by many as friendly animals that can co-habit with man suitably.

When it comes to pets, they are esteemed in most countries of the world. They are human's best companions. They are an integral part of our modern society as they easily adapt to the living conditions of men. The dog walking business is one of many businesses that have continued to stem from dogs. This dog-walking business is such that have and would continue to flourish for a long time to come.

The dog walking business is something any kid who loves pets and wants to make some pocket-money might be excited to take on. It is a venture that gives any child an opportunity to enjoy himself while making money. It is a clear case of getting paid for what you love doing.

Hence, one can conclude that the dog walking business is a money spinner as it has continued to yield profits for those that engage in it. As a Dog owner, walking dog is part of the responsibilities of keeping a dog as there will always be the need for dogs to take walks, because of the numerous health benefits, as well as the feeling it gives the dogs. The business thrives because most dog owners are busy as they may have little or no time at all to spare to walk their dogs. Although there are dog professional walkers indeed in the industry, it cannot be said that it is a saturated industry. In reality, the number of dog walkers is still small compared to the population of people who own dog pets

Becoming a dog walker isn't a difficult task, as you don't need to get a certification whatsoever. All that you need is a love for pet animals, as well as the time to walk the animals around.

Understand the Industry

The Dog Walking business is a fast-growing business as pet owners increase daily. So many people still see pets more steadily as members of the family which make it easier for anyone to get dog walking job. You can easily find families in need of a dog walker. It often pays more money than pet sitting and can become a regular job for a youngster. Furthermore, some households own more than one pet. This is one of the good reasons why people in the dog-walking business make good money.

Know the Major players in the Industry

The dog walking industry can boast of well-known brands that have grown from a small level to become household names.

The industry has recorded a great level of success since its inception. Here are some of the popular dog-walking companies; Dog Walkers

- Trauma Service Dogs
- Warrior Canine
- Passivity Dog Services
- Wow Dog Walkers

you can check the internet for more

Economic prospect

Dog walking is a business that would not cost you much to start. You do not need a huge startup capital because you aren't into production but service rendering. Therefore, it is a business one can start with not too big a capital.

The only thing is that you may need to spend little to promote your business.

Just like every other business, you will need to create awareness about your dog walking services. One of the best ways to promote the business is using flyers and business cards. Make professional business cards and flyers that you can distribute to people to advertise your dog walking services.

Know the Threats and Challenges you are likely to face in the business

Dog walking business just like any other business has got its fair share of threats and challenges. As a young entrepreneur, you should prepare adequately for this.

Here are some of the challenging situations and how to handle them.

Unfavorable Weather

Dogs may also need to be walked when the weather is not favorable.

It may be cold, snowing, or raining. It's therefore, a good idea for you to know some basic first aid treatments for canines, such as treating a dog that gets a cut on its paw.

It is also good to know how to keep dogs cool to prevent overheating in harsh weather.

Aggressive dogs

You should walk your dogs in well-lit and well-populated areas that you know very well, watching out for cars, avoiding aggressive dogs, and fast-moving bicycles.

Don't allow your dog to run into the street without proper supervision, and avoid other dogs and their owners until you know both dogs are friendly and can relate.

Choose a Catchy Business Name

You must adopt a very charming name for your dog-walking business. You have to be creative with it so that whatever name you choose to adopt reflects the services you offer.

Find out about the Best Insurance Policies for your New Business

You need insurance covers for your business. The good thing is that there are several insurance policies available for the dog walking business. You must choose a plan that will work best for your business. You may consider discussing with an expert whom you will work closely with to put you through.

Write a Business Plan full of ideas and Strategies

Running a business successfully requires writing a well-thought-out plan on how to run the business. This will make you realize that starting a business indeed is a serious task that must be taken seriously.

Several things must be incorporated into the plan. The good news is that, if you do not know something, there are people out there to help you. You can easily engage a business plan writer, whom you will supply all the vital information to put together a standard business plan for you. You should note that these professional consultants do not do this for free, so be prepared to offer a fee.

Your business plan must include the following information.

- The aim of starting the business
- Your marketing strategies
- How you want to run your business
- The number of employees that are required to start

- Short-term and long-term goals for your business, and so on.

Using the right marketing channels that work will help in getting clients for the business.

Your plan must include an effective marketing strategy from the beginning.

It will be difficult getting people to know about your business if this aspect is lacking from the beginning.

You have to do some research on what work best in the industry. You can find out from those already in the business, how they have been able to manage the situation.

You can also contact a business consultant to help you brainstorm on possible means of reaching your target client.

Here are some marketing strategies that you can choose to advertise your dog-walking business

- Create professional business cards and handbills that advertise your dog walking services. Make sure that the bill/cards contain attractive photos of dogs and contact information of your location.
- Advertise in business directories. and business magazines.
- List your business on the yellow pages
- Build a website to promote your dog walking business.
- Advertise on social media, radio stations, and TV stations.

The Cost to Start the Business

As earlier stated, setting up a dog walking business might not require much money, but the truth is that it will cost you something.

You will need to spend a little on the following

- The Amount needed to acquire a suitable Office facility in a business district
- The required licenses
- The registration of your business
- The location you will operate
- The cost of equipping your office

Raise the Needed Startup Capital

Raising adequate startup capital can be very challenging for a young entrepreneur.

You can source capital if you don't have sufficient savings to start.

There are various ways through which you can source funds to start your dream business.

Here are some of the means by which you can generate money for your business;

You can raise money from

- savings business partners
- business partners

- personal stocks
- A loan from your Bank/banks
- Applying for business grants
- Angel investors
- family members and friends
-

Choose a Suitable Location

You need a good base to operate, a suitable place where people can meet you to discuss business. Although it is a dog-walking business, you need a place to do the talking before the walking.

The place does not necessarily need to be flamboyant, but it has to be well-equipped.

Just as we know dogs live mainly in residents than in corporate settings. Therefore, choosing a residential neighborhood will be a very good option.

In addition, the location must be in the main town of the city. The office should contain different units, like; the reception where guests are received, a store where the pet foods and other relevant items are stored as well as the sick bay, where a vet doctor can check out the pets when they are ill.

Your office should contain internet-enabled computers, furniture, and a host of other fittings and decoration that would make your office a befitting place.

Engage people for your Technical and Manpower Needs

As time goes on and you scale up your dog walking business, you would need other employees that would occupy various strategic positions such as; managers, supervisors, clerks, dog walkers, vet doctors, and so on. A medium-sized dog-walking business requires a total of 7 – 10 employees to run.

Create a Corporate Identity

It is a competitive business you have to develop iron-clad competitive strategies to keep you on the job

There are numerous ways through which you can surpass your competitors to survive in the business. One of the ways is by coming up with various innovations to win the hearts of clients.

You may decide to treat the dogs when you observe they are not well. You can groom them, train them on some etiquette and render other extra services to make your business stand out.

.

Work on ways you can keep your clients.

Keep the quality high **and be consistent in your services.** Keep training your workers so that your business can maintain a standard operating process without declining to keep your customers. Once your customers suspect that the quality of your services has dropped, they may begin to look for alternative services. Ensure that all your clients are given the best treatments at all time.

Develop a procedure to make all the members of your team have to go the extra mile in caring for and protecting the dogs that are in their care.

Spend time interacting with the dog you'll be walking with before you lunch out getting to know your new friend helps you to bond with him and understand his personality to make the job easier. Try to see if the dog interacts well with other animals and people so you'll know how best to handle him. It will help you to determine what to avoid when you walk him.

Ask the dog owner for a cell phone number so you can quickly make a contact if you have any sudden challenging issues that arise with the dogs. Let your parents be on standby as a backup to handle emergencies.

5.Pet sitting Business

Figure 4 Pet sitting

Pet sitting business, just like dog walking business is one of the most flourishing business endeavors for a kid. It is another brilliant way to earn extra money at a young age. If you are a pet lover then this is quite a good business to invest in as it helps you to turn your passion into a profitable venture. It is a fun exercise that helps you maintain interest by doing something you cherish and at the same time make money.

The pet-sitting business is a less laborious job but highly fulfilling and rewarding at the same time. It can teach kids patience, cooperation, and responsibility. The good news about the business is that you can still do some other things and earn extra money with it.

Pros of a Pet-Sitting Business

Low start-up cost: The start-up cost of the business is low as it doesn't require much capital to start. The start-up cost is limited and small. All you need to do is to get some basic pet supplies. The good thing is that in most cases, the pet owners will provide you with the supplies themselves like leashes or dog food or the toys which their pet prefers in most cases.

Low time commitment: The job will not take too much of your time as you only need a limited amount of time to feed, water, and exercise the animal.

Additionally, you may not need to hire or rent an office to operate. Most of what you do will be at the pet owner's home or in the public area where you care for the pet.

Pet sitting business doesn't have to be full-time work; it is a business you can do as a side job to earn some extra income. It can be combined with other commitments.

Availability of Customers: It is quite easy to get customers within your neighborhood as you can reach your clients in so many ways. You can advertise or get into contact with close pet stores or veterinarians who will in turn refer customers to you.

Cons of a Pet-Sitting Business

Although, formal training is not required for pet sitting, but you do need to have some amount of knowledge and expertise to deal with multiple pets or breeds. You will need different approach to attend to different dog behavior.

Conflicting times: Pet sitting schedules may coincide with your family planned vacations. As a result, your family traveling plans may be delayed or altered, because many families travel while schools are on vacation. You may not go on vacation as you plan as you need to adjust your time to satisfy your clients.

High level of Responsibility: You might need to have more than an average level of physical fitness and energy due to the high level of responsibility demand by the job,

You will be caring for animals, if you are not strong or you neglect certain aspects of their care, you can face terrible consequences.

You must be fit to keep up with a lot of pets at one given time because every animal has a different nature or character

You may need to get insurance or bonding in case of liability. Although, it is not compulsory, but it is recommended for you because it is possible you lose the pet or he gets injured. The owner can become very upset and sue you for your negligence. Getting insurance or bonding will help see you through the challenging period.

Tips for setting up a pet-sitting business for kids:

Consider the Responsibility: You have to critically examine the gravity of the responsibility because taking care of pets is a huge task.

Make sure you understand what the task is all about and equip yourself adequately. It will be a good idea to have an adult preferably your parents who can guide you through your pet-sitting career.

Small Beginning: Pet sitting business requires that you don't start in a big way so that you don't burn your fingers quickly and become discouraged. It is always a good idea to start slowly and move steadily with time. Perhaps you can start with one family to acquire the necessary experience and become comfortable with your new role. You can then gradually expand the business so that you have plenty of time to provide quality care and attention to each pet.

Advertise: Reach out to people to let them know about your business by advertising. It is a good idea to start with your friends, family, and neighbors.

Make posters and business cards and circulate them to create awareness in the community. Make sure you use an adult's phone number on the cards and create an email address solely for your pet-sitting business

Start by giving your business a charming name and make sure it reflects the services you offer. Display your flyers and posters on the bulletin board in local businesses and at dog parks and leave your business card at the veterinarian's clinic.

Figure 5perfect Bonding

Visit the family before the first pet-sitting

It's important to meet with the family and interact with the pet in front of the family before taking on the responsibility of handling the pet alone. This action will likely make the pet feel more at ease with you and begin to develop a trusting relationship with you fast as a pet sitter.

At this meeting time make sure you understand clearly the family expectation. This is very crucial as you will know how best to handle the pet in line with the family's expectations.

Some pet owners prefer to leave a binder or checklist prepared and email in advance.

If the family is not providing a checklist, then prepare copious notes and then review the notes with an adult before discussing with the family to take up the pet-sitting job.

Visiting the family before the first pet-sitting visit is very important. It will help you to have all the important contact numbers of the family including their family veterinarian, and any close-by relatives.

6 Online Business Ideas for Kids and Teens

Online business is a great way for young entrepreneurs to earn money without ever needing to leave the comfort of their homes.

If you have the tech skills and resources, this is much easier than other business that needs a fixed location.

The Internet is a good platform for selling homemade products and services.

It offers a great opportunity for kids who want to earn money from their creative works such as art, crafts, and, writing. It allows you to reach a wide range of audience.

Here are some suggestions to start building an online store and make it successful.

The good way to start is to first make a list of your hobbies and see the one you can easily turn into a money-making venture. You have to decide whether you want to sell a physical product or a digital product. Both are available online. When you have decided on the idea you want to sell. You need to do **some research to see if your business idea will sell.** If you are satisfied with your findings, next you want to brainstorm how you can make your product or services unique, high quality, and desirable.

Search for similar products and see if it is doing well. Note the design and see how you can improve on it.

Next, you want to create a business name for your brand. You have to come up with catchy descriptive brand names that people will easily remember.

Don't forget to always write appropriate product descriptions for what you want to sell. This is very vital; it is the product description that will give people insight into what you are selling, so you must write it very well.

In setting your prices, you have to consider the cost of production and the price of similar products. Don't overcharge so that you don't scare your customers. It is equally vital that you don't undercharge so that you don't cheat yourself.

Make sure your price is pocket friendly to your customers, and also fair to you.

Here are some ways you can set up an online business.

Selling on Etsy Store

Etsy is an online store stuffed with the creations of individual vendors. If you want to sell artisan products of any kind, this is a good place to go to display your product online.

Setting up an Etsy online shop is easy.

This can be done in these 5 simple steps

Step1

The first step is to go to Etsy and set your shop preferences (country and currency)

Step 2

The next step is to name your shop (you can search for available names)

Step 3

Next, you want to stock your shop by dropping the pictures of your items for sale.

Step 4

Next, you set up the customer payment methods

Step 5

Complete the process by setting up how you'll want to get paid

A lot of videos are available on YouTube on how to get this done in minutes.

.

Etsy takes care of all the payment details and the storefront on their website, but you are the one to decide the amount to sell the product and the locations for shipping. In doing this task, you have to consider other expenses involved. For instance Etsy charge ($0.20 per item sold) and for online payments. You have to take care of packing and shipping, which of course becomes part of your additional start-up cost.

You must note that you have to market your product to drive traffic to your store.

Self-Publish Your Books

You can publish your book at print on demand sites. They are sites that help you to publish your written works such as **novels, storybooks, and poems** and share them with the world.

Once your work is ready go to their site and upload following the stated guidelines and your work is published. Thereafter, you need to monitor your sales and wait to be paid. The hosting website prints on demand and ships to the customer once an order is made.

Creating an Online Course

There are several ways to offer your knowledge-based business online You can sell your knowledge by creating how-to or instructions for sale. You need to record instruction videos step by step to teach others. Once you have created your content, then you can employ some of the course hosting websites.

7. Final Thoughts

Entrepreneurship can be started at a young age. Starting your own business not only teaches you responsibility, but it gives you valuable life skills that you can use in adulthood. It also gives you opportunity to make money which you can save or invest for future uses.